Good Vibes

Coloring Book For Teens

Copyright 2020 by Happy Harper - All rights reserved.

This document is geared towards providing exact and reliable information in regards to the topic and issue covered. The publication is sold with the idea that the publisher is not required to render an accounting, officially permitted, or otherwise, qualified services. If advice is necessary, legal or professional, a practiced individual in the profession should be ordered.

- From a Declaration of Principles which was accepted and approved equally by a Committee of the American Bar Association and a Committee of Publishers and Associations.

In no way is it legal to reproduce, duplicate, or transmit any part of this document by either electronic means or in printed format. Recording of this publication is strictly prohibited and any storage of this document is not allowed unless with written permission from the publisher. All rights reserved.

The information provided herein is stated to be truthful and consistent, in that any liability, in terms of inattention or otherwise, by any usage or abuse of any policies, processes, or directions contained within is the solitary and utter responsibility of the recipient reader. Under no circumstances will any legal responsibility or blame be held against the publisher for any reparation, damages, or monetary loss due to the information herein, either directly or indirectly.

Respective authors and companies own all copyrights not held by the publisher.

The information herein is offered for informational purposes solely and is universal as so. The presentation of the information is without a contract or any type of guarantee assurance.

The trademarks that are used are without any consent, and the publication of the trademark is without permission or backing by the trademark owner. All trademarks and brands within this book are for clarifying purposes only and are owned by the owners themselves, not affiliated with this document.

This Book Belongs to

_____

YOU ARE STRONGER than you THINK

YOU ARE STRONGER than you THINK

Great job on coloring all the pages!

As a thank you for purchasing this book, enjoy these bonus coloring pages from one of our other coloring books!

A Message From the Publisher

Hello! My name is Harper and I am the owner of Happy Harper Publishing, the publishing house that brought you this title.

My hope is that your little one loved this book and enjoyed each and every page. If they did, please think about leaving a review for us on Amazon or wherever you purchased this book. It may only take a moment, but it really does mean the world for small businesses like mine.

The mission of Happy Harper is to create premium content for children that will help them learn new things, grow their imaginations, improve their motor skills, and have lots of fun doing it. Without you, however, this would not be possible, so we sincerely thank you for your purchase and for supporting our company mission.

~ Harper

Check out our other books!

For more, visit our Amazon store at:
amazon.com/author/happyharper

www.ingramcontent.com/pod-product-compliance
Lightning Source LLC
Chambersburg PA
CBHW081157070526
44583CB00021B/2882